ONCE UPON A RHYME

IMAGINATION FOR A NEW GENERATION

Warwickshire

Edited by Heather Killingray

First published in Great Britain in 2004 by:
Young Writers
Remus House
Coltsfoot Drive
Peterborough
PE2 9JX
Telephone: 01733 890066
Website: www.youngwriters.co.uk

SB ISBN 1 84460 506 X

Foreword

Young Writers was established in 1991 and has been passionately devoted to the promotion of reading and writing in children and young adults ever since. The quest continues today. Young Writers remains as committed to engendering the fostering of burgeoning poetic and literary talent as ever.

This year's Young Writers competition has proven as vibrant and dynamic as ever and we are delighted to present a showcase of the best poetry from across the UK. Each poem has been carefully selected from a wealth of *Once Upon A Rhyme* entries before ultimately being published in this, our twelfth primary school poetry series.

Once again, we have been supremely impressed by the overall high quality of the entries we have received. The imagination, energy and creativity which has gone into each young writer's entry made choosing the best poems a challenging and often difficult but ultimately hugely rewarding task - the general high standard of the work submitted amply vindicating this opportunity to bring their poetry to a larger appreciative audience.

We sincerely hope you are pleased with our final selection and that you will enjoy *Once Upon A Rhyme Warwickshire* for many years to come.

Contents

Laura Beatrice Woodfield (10)	34
Oliver Rose (9)	35
Jacob Lindley (10)	36
Ryan Birch (11)	37
Robert Stuart Lilley (11)	38
Jack Waller (11)	39
Bethan Payne (9)	40
Charlotte Holmes (9)	41
Jasmine Faulkner-Gant (9)	42
Rosie Sheppard (8)	43
Bradley Sheppard (10)	44
Ben Faulkner-Gant (11)	45

Great Alne Primary School

Jack Blackman (9)	46
Scarlett Madge (11)	47
Holly Varnish (9)	48
Sarah Miriam Burch (11)	49
Alex Horgan (10)	50
Kathryn Major (11)	51
Marianne Piotrowski (11)	52
Jovita West (10)	53
Jack Dunbar (8)	54
Rachel Moore (8)	55
Jacob Turner (7)	56
Hannah Smardon (10)	57

Middlemarch School

Emma Proctor (11)	58
Kelly Cooper (10)	59
Rosie Kinder (10)	60
Mitchell Ward (10)	61
Mollie Rice (8)	62
Rhian Gemma Moore (8)	63
Liam Betteridge (10)	64
Steven Sadhara (8)	65
Samantha Walker (9)	66
Elizabeth Anne Proctor (10)	67
Laura Lapper (10)	68

Our Lady's Catholic Primary School

Jessica Quinn-Dobbins (9)	69
Charlie Jayne Stanley (10)	70
Shannon Hall (10)	71
Rachel Hendry (10)	72
Anthony Kendall (10)	73
Samantha Preece (10)	74
James Dyer (9)	75
Daisy Ann Gisbourne (10)	76
Christian Hall (10)	77
Amy Rose Bingham (10)	78
Lucie Jade Watson (10)	79
Tessa Smallbone (11)	80
Emily Atherton (10)	81
Danielle Kessey (11)	82
Jenny Roberts (10)	83
Rory Kavanagh (10)	84
Chloe Shaw (11)	85
Michael Bennett (10)	86
Arthur Bennett (10)	87

St Faith's CE Junior School, Alcester

Amelia Hopkins (9)	88
Charlotte Howl (10)	89
Jack Miles (10)	90
Adam Woollacott (10)	91
Matthew Laight (10)	92
Ben Smith (11)	93
Chris Hodge (10)	94
Lucy Sloan (9)	95
Eleanor Reeves (9)	96
Jamie Glenn (10)	97
Sean Blyth (9)	98
Mae Yee Chek (10)	99
Samantha Richards (10)	100
Sophie Bird (10)	101
Charlotte Maycock (10)	102
Katie Hand (11)	103
Patrick Sarson (10)	104
Peter Bridgeford (9)	105
April Hands (9)	106

Katie Hoskins (10)   107
Joseph Rawlings (9)   108
Ellie O'Shea (10)   109
Lauren Matheson (10)   110
Laura Morris (11)   111
Penny Sreeves (9)   112
Jamie Done (10)   113
Eloise Bonehill (10)   114

St Francis RC Primary School, Bedworth
Jared Wigmore (9)   115
Kerry Louise O'Connor (9)   116
Laura Wilthew (10)   117
Sarah Atkins (9)   118
Roseanne Howard (9)   119
Scott Harris (9)   120
Arandeep Hayer (9)   121
MIchael McDade (10)   122
Joseph Dell (9)   123
Ryan Michael Keane (10)   124
Daniel Smith-Walker (9)   125
Steven Haddon (9)   126
Jessica Neale (9)   127
Sophie Neale (9)   128
Laura James (10)   129
Charlotte Burkinshaw (10)   130
James Ingleston (9)   131
Ross O' Donoghue (9)   132
Lucinda Batchelor (9)   133
Thomas Moore (10)   134

St Mary's RC Primary School, Studley
Madeleine Glasbey (9)   135
Grace Lynskey (8)   136
Elizabeth Edgar (8)   137

St Nicholas' CE Primary School, Kenilworth
Rose Allcock (10)   138
Ella Hall (11)   139
Joanne Marshall (10)   140

Georgina Eastaugh (10)   141
Isabel Sturt (10)   142
Bethany Thorne (9)   143
Georgia Sturt (8)   144
Megan Edgington (10)   145
Jacob Mansbridge (11)   146
Ben Moseley (9)   147
Gregory Hulme (10)   148
Nathan Wood (11)   149

St Peter's CE Primary School, Market Bosworth
Joshua Bonser (10)   150
Joe Duckney (10)   151
Sophie Lacey (6)   152
Ceri Norton (11)   153
Helena Parkes (7)   154
Callum Denore (7)   155
Mahin Kohli (10)   156
Lucy Mary Fallon (8)   157
Chloe McDougall (7)   158
Grace Woolmer (8)   159
George Bassnett (10)   160
Hannah Jackson (9)   161
Michael Maguire (10)   162
Lucy Sandford-James (7)   163
Anna Sandford-James (7)   164
Ellie Hicklin (11)   165
Sophie Powell (11)   166
Joseph Rowland (9)   167
Mike Titley (10)   168
Gemma Steel (10)   169
Annabelle Saunders (8)   170
Chloe Lockett (10)   171
Alex Coney (10)   172
Rachel Naylor (11)   173
Danielle Aucott (9)   174
Fiona Naylor (8)   175
Sabina Marr (8)   176
Emily Roberts (8)   177

Shrubland Street Community Prmary School

Leah Croston (9)	178
Victoria Brown (10)	179
Jade Reeve (10)	180
Rebekah Waterfield (9)	181
Anja Bell (10)	182
Thomas Hood (10)	183
Harriet Bartle (11)	184
Joe Durrant (11)	185
Zac Chandler (10)	186
Joseph Kwasnik (11)	187
Siani Cox (11)	188
Rachel Hannah Brook (10)	189
Aneesha Doal (10)	190

The Poems

Box Of Love

There's a box,
a box of love
sitting in the centre
of the table.
The outside
is decorated with
a verse of a poem.
The poem
is of love.
You open the box
and inside are
pictures of love
on a heart
which is yours.
But one thing
catches your eye
and that is
a song.
The song of your
dreams
and a man
is singing it
and the love
is locked in
until your
love life is
complete.

Lauren Manning (11)
Abbots Farm Junior School

Autumn

A corns are being collected by squirrels rushing about
U nderfoot leaves crackle as you walk to school
T reetops sway from side to side
U nder the soil it is wet
M y hair blows back as if it is running away
N ew days begin in autumn.

Megan Jones (7)
Abbots Farm Junior School

First Frost

The frost falls upon us
like a cat pouncing on its prey.
Plants are dying from the freezing frost,
the ground is visible no more.
Gradually frost takes over autumn.
The leaves turn to crisp,
making a magical sight for people passing by.
Frost is magical!

Bethany Whittle (9)
Abbots Farm Junior School

The Thing That Might Be There

My dog is barking at something.
What would he be barking at?
I can't see anything outside,
Another dog, a cat?

Maybe we know them
Yes! One of our friendly folk
Or maybe it's a stranger
A killer in a cloak!

I will take my chances
I'll open up the door
But what if I end up
Unconscious on the floor?

'Mum!' I shout desperately
I think she cannot hear
'There's something scary outside!'
My end is very near.

I hide under a cushion
Then under the table instead
I think I need a better hiding place,
I tiptoe upstairs and slip under my *bed!*

Taylor Reid (10)
Abbots Farm Junior School

The Eagle's Hunt

Sharp eyes like diamonds, scanning the ground,
Searching for prey,
Golden wings, vanishing into the horizon,
A beak like a butcher's knife, ripping meat apart,
Just waiting to strike, once again,
Mice retreated to corners, struggling to escape,
Gone in the blink of an eye.

Sam Back (9) & Reece Abrams (10)
Abbots Farm Junior School

Dogs

As I walk through the park,
This scary dog attacks me.
My legs turn to jelly,
My body turns to ice.

He runs at me, as fast as a cheetah,
The world around me seems like a blur.
The dog is brown, like chocolate
And as frightening as a thunderstorm.

I try to run,
But my legs are glued to the ground.
I want to move, but I can't.
I watch as the dog gnashes his teeth.

Natalie Round (10)
Abbots Farm Junior School

Happiness

If happiness were a colour it would be yellow.
If happiness were a food it would be sweets.
If happiness were a piece of clothing it would be a nice,
warm sweater.
If happiness were a car, it would be a BMW.
If happiness were a country it would be America.
If happiness were a song it would be a song of love.
If happiness were an animal it would be a rabbit.
If happiness were a shape it would be a star.
If happiness were a treat it would be a trip to Disneyland, Florida.
If happiness were a flower it would be a daffodil.

Lee Gibson (10)
Abbots Farm Junior School

Cats

Sleek, scratching cats
Scary to me, cute to you.
Walking along the quiet street
Staring, staring.
No blink, I shiver.
'Stay away,' I say.
Closer, closer
It gains.
Hooking its eyes on me,
Licking its lips.
I'm thinking, *I'm dinner*
Stretching out its paws
I wish the ground would suck me up,
Or I would be transported home,
Or slide down a plug hole and up into my bed.
The pressure lies on me,
What will it do?
What will I do?
That's why I hate cats!

Mayuri Patel (9)
Abbots Farm Junior School

Blazing Colours

Bye-bye summer, hello autumn,
Blazing colours,
Golden red, yellow and brown,
This is my season.

I love it,
Acorns are falling,
Conkers are bashing,
This is my true love.

Colourful as the golden sunset,
The leaves are getting browner,
The plums are being harvested.
Oh yes, I love this, oh yes I do!

David McGott (10)
Abbots Farm Junior School

Spider In The Bath

I found a spider in the bath,
It really didn't make me laugh.
I cried and cried and called my mum,
But she was out, she couldn't come.

The spider was so big and hairy,
It really was extremely scary.
I cried and cried and called my mum,
But she was out, she didn't come.

I felt so scared, I stood stock-still,
The spider made me feel quite ill.
I cried and cried and called my mum,
But she was out, she didn't come.

The spider started to crawl towards me,
I closed my eyes so I would not see.
I cried and cried and called my mum -
And she was back - she *did* come!

Rachel Stanley (9)
Abbots Farm Junior School

Box Of Nightmares

As I rest upon my bed
and night draws nigh,
a black box appears next to me,
then slowly opens
and the contents fill
my head.
As I drift to sleep,
I can hear
the drip, drip, dripping of blood,
the hair-raising scream of a banshee.
I can smell
rotten bodies from beneath the floorboards,
musty breath.
Mum says
it's in my mind
so the
drip, drip, dripping of blood
must be a leaky tap,
the hair-raising scream
must be the wind.
But Mum can't
explain the smell.
I wonder!

Megan Harding (11)
Abbots Farm Junior School

Box Of Nightmares

Deep down in my cellar
behind the old kitchen door
lies the small wooden box
as black as the night sky
crammed full of nightmares!
Inside the box is the Devil
who hides in our nightmares.
Nightmares of turning into a werewolf,
of being chased by something.
Of the bogeyman.
But these nightmares should never,
never ever be revealed to the world
to once again reign with their terror amongst us.
A box to be opened only with care.

Luke Horrocks (11)
Abbots Farm Junior School

Box Of Nightmares

In my box of nightmares
with elephants carved all round,
my scariest ever dreams
are kept safe and sound.
The one with the floorboards creaking
and lightning crashing down.
The shivers down my spine
and the whispers of the wind.
Someone walking behind you, breathing
heavily on your back
and dripping of water.
Nails scraping down the blackboard
and monsters, ghosts and ghouls.
Now I will not have to worry again,
thanks to the box,
they are kept safely away.

Ellie Michael (10)
Abbots Farm Junior School

Box Of Unknown Treasures

This morning,
I awoke to see a large cardboard box
Lying beside my bed.
　　It was:
Painted by a rainbow
And covered by riches from faraway lands.
　　I listened,
I could hear the fluttering of wings.
Was there a creature inside?
　　I looked,
A miraculous golden light streamed into my eyes.
Was it a box of colour or wishes?
　　I smelt,
The smell of melted chocolate filled the room.
Maybe it was treats from Grandma?
　　I felt,
I felt pearls, their delicate, smooth, round bodies of different sizes.
They could be from India.
　　I wondered,
What's in this box of unknown treasures?
I had no idea . . .

　　So I opened it.

Shelley Parry (11)
Abbots Farm Junior School

Box Of Colours

In the box
where colours swirl
and mix
a rainbow holds our colours.
Pink love,
blue cries,
gold joy,
red evil,
green nature.
They're all held
by one rainbow
the colours
of the world.
And there they are stored
until the rainbow escapes
and the colours
of the world
are scattered.

Kelly Suggett (10)
Abbots Farm Junior School

My Brother

My brother is tall and thin,
He can beat me,
But I usually win.
He is as boring as a bug,
I hate it when he gives me a huge hug.
He never goes to school,
Or in a swimming pool.
He just stays in bed
But normally knocks me on the head.

Corey Thomas (8)
Abbots Farm Junior School

Winter

I hear it now, what is it?
I think it's the wind whistling through my ear,
I see snowflakes falling in the snow like little twinkling stars,
I feel the snowflakes melting on my tongue,
Slippery ice makes me fall down
And when the day is over, winter will be gone.

Brodie Pond (8)
Abbots Farm Junior School

My Brother

My brother is small and cuddly,
His blond hair as gold as the sun's rays,
To him I must be very tall and brave,
My mum says to me, 'You must teach him how to behave.'

My brother is as funny as a circus clown,
His eyes are big and blue, like precious sapphires,
We play outside when it is sunny and hot,
We two brothers love each other such a lot.

Joshua Checkley (8)
Abbots Farm Junior School

Happy

If happiness were a place it would be Florida
going on all the rides.
If happiness were a colour it would be yellow
to light up the world.
If happiness were a car it would be a Lotus
racing along the road.
If happiness were a tree it would be an oak tree
standing up tall.
If happiness were a book it would be a love story
to make you happy.
If happiness were a person it would be my teacher, Mr Wolsey
being kind to everyone.

If happiness were a funny person it would be a clown
fooling about.
If happiness were a bright light it would be the sun
shimmering.
But the thing that makes us all happy is
Friends!

Jake Pogson (8)
Abbots Farm Junior School

World War

W ar is so harsh,
O ver a million people get killed,
R ushing ambulances everywhere,
L oads of people getting trapped under homes,
D ynamite and bombs killing thousands,

W hat if war could just stop,
A nd everybody could be friends?
R ather we had a peaceful world than a world of war.

Sarah Osborne (10)
Alveston CE Primary School

Fusion

Fusion brings people together
Fusion brings my thoughts together
Fusion brings wires, batteries,
Lights and other parts to make a circuit
Fusion brings the world together.

Nathan Smith (10)
Alveston CE Primary School

Ice Hockey

I ce flying up at my face like shrapnel
C ome on, let's score a goal!
E dging towards the net.

H ang on, yes, it's in!
O h, what a goal
C ome on!
K ind of excited now
E xcellent, we're winning by two
Y es, we've won, we've bagged the game.

Alex Young (11)
Alveston CE Primary School

Rugby

R unning about with the ball, going towards the try-line.
U sing my kicking tee to kick over the posts.
G reat kick, over the post it goes.
B ig, large boy running at me.
Y ou panic and wonder what to do.

Andrew Mole (10)
Alveston CE Primary School

The Spring Bloom

Daffodils shooting up in the air,
The baby animals waking for the first time,
The summer breeze beginning to blow,
The blossom starting to grow on the trees,
Spring is here at last.

Hayley Allman (10)
Alveston CE Primary School

Racing

Bikes
Racing round the track.
Screeching
Skidding round the marked track.
Knee pads
Scraping the inner track.
Number 10
Zoomed past the finish line.
Happily pulled back
A fantastic wheelie and the crowd rose.
The crowd
Clapped out of *joy*
And the biker waved back.

Alex Batsford (10)
Alveston CE Primary School

Summer's Over

Summer is when children come out to play
Summer is when the sun comes out to shine
But it is almost over now
Will it hold on for a little longer?
Temperature dropping
Autumn is near
Leaves dying
Ready to fall.

Jason Sellar (10)
Alveston CE Primary School

Once Upon A Rhyme . . .

Oil was purple and pink,
Nails could speak and think,
Cats wore dresses and fancy shoes,
Elephants and birds came in twos.
Umbrellas went to school,
Pigs and cows played football,
Ostriches had arms and faces,
Nightingales carried cases.
Ants were silver and blue,
Rabbits barked and went *moo,*
Horses had no teeth and hair,
Yo-yos played 'truth or dare',
Mountains could walk,
Eggs could dance and talk . . .

India Ouseley (10)
Ettington Primary School

Once Upon A Rhyme

Once upon a rhyme
a super sneaky spy by the name of Joseph Time
was told that the Knave of Hearts
who stole the tarts
now wanted to steal the secret of rhyme.
He planned to put Humpty Dumpty on the great wall
so that he had a great fall.
The Knave of Hearts
who stole the tarts
will steal Humpty's secret of rhyme,
he will be committing a crime,
if he's caught it will cost him more than a dime!
It's the job of Joseph Time to save the secret of rhyme
and catch the Knave of Hearts
who stole the tarts
and save Humpty from a great fall
off the great wall.
Super, sneaky, spy, Joseph Time
went to the door across the moorland
and arrive in Rhyme Land
He put down his trampoline next to the great wall
to save Humpty Dumpty from a great fall.
Humpty Dumpty sat on the wall
the Knave of Hearts who stole the tarts let off some fireworks,
Humpty Dumpty had a great fall
but landed on Joseph's trampoline
and bounced onto the Knave of Hearts
who stole the tarts
and all the king's horses and all the king's men
arrested the Knave of Hearts
who stole the tarts.
The secret of the rhyme was safe.

Joseph Lucas (9)
Ettington Primary School

Lost Fairy

The fairy kingdom was all sweet and sound.
In forget-me-nots blue, a baby was found.
With red rosy cheeks and long blonde hair.
No necklaces, no head bands, her whole face was bare.
Up in the trees a woman sat,
And her little hands were making a hat.
'My daughter, my daughter,' she would cry.
Her hands outstretched and a tear in her eye.
I handed her daughter back to her arms
And left for the palace thinking of charms.
It was eight o'clock so I climbed into bed.
Within five minutes I had laid back my head.

Bethan Lindley (8)
Ettington Primary School

Once Upon A Rhyme . . . !

Once upon a rhyme . . .
We all sat down to dine;
We combed the dogs for fleas,
Which we added to the peas;
We got feathers from the birds,
Which we mixed up with some herbs;
Then we all had cups of Coke,
Which we flavoured with old soap;
We gutted seven pigs,
Which we ate with mouldy figs;
We cooked a rat's left eye,
Which tasted lovely in the pie;
After pudding - spotted dick -
We all felt rather sick;
So we left a massive slice,
Which we boiled with some mice;
Which we really thought we should,
Give to Edwards, Emms and Goode!

Lucy Allen (9)
Ettington Primary School

My Friends

My friends are cool,
And we play ball,
And our team is the best.

We never fight,
Over who is right,
And always beat the rest.

When things go bad,
And I am sad,
They cheer me up and cheer me on.

They are always there,
And always fair,
In Stratford-upon-Avon.

Alexander Marney (9)
Ettington Primary School

Once Upon A Rhyme

Once upon a rhyme
No one drank wine,
It was always lime
Day in day out.

Once upon a rhyme
Everything was mine,
Until the time
Came to nine.

Once upon a rhyme
Everything went fine,
When up popped a sign
Made of pine.

Once upon a rhyme
People worked till nine,
They never had time to drink lime
Or even wine.

Thomas Marshall (9)
Ettington Primary School

Once Upon A Rhyme

Once upon a rhyme,
I stepped back in time,
The Earth was a better place then,
People were not herded into a pen,
Nature was much happier,
Life and people were less snappier,
The only two things that I think are better
Are technology and healthcare,
Let's keep these and go back there.

Jamie Widdowson **(11)**
Ettington Primary School

Once Upon A Rhyme . . .

Once upon a rhyme,
I picked some thyme,
It went well with lime!

My favourite author is Anne Fine,
Want a glass of wine?
What's happened to the washing line?

Once upon a rhyme,
I picked some thyme,
It went well with lime!

Sometimes I take the time,
And watch people mime,
I want a Dime.

Once upon a rhyme,
I picked some thyme,
It went well with lime!

Laura Beatrice Woodfield (10)
Ettington Primary School

Once Upon A Rhyme

Once upon a rhyme
I looked at the time
it was time to feed the cat.

The cat had a rat
it came in through the flap.

The food was put down
but the cat said, 'Yuck!'

Oliver Rose (9)
Ettington Primary School

It's A Wonder

Dragon red, dragon fire,
dragons do not make me tire . . .
Dragons are amazing creatures,
they have the most astonishing features!
Spikes of gold, wings of blue,
scales of green and they tower huge . . . !

Jacob Lindley (10)
Ettington Primary School

Once Upon A Rhyme

Once in good times
A man made some rhymes
He sat on a rock all day
Thinking how to say . . .

Homework is so long
If only it could be more fun
If it was shorter
We could get the job done.

On a cold Wednesday
While he was in the hay
A thought came into his head
Why don't we do this instead?

Beg the teachers for less
While we are in Loch Ness
Then it won't be so boring
Because we can do some talking.

'Success, success!' all the children shouted.
'We have persuaded them to abort this
The teachers have given us a shortage
Because they have allowed us to be talkative.'

Ryan Birch (11)
Ettington Primary School

Once Upon A Rhyme

Once upon a rhyme,
I took a little time,
And I wrote a poem about a goat.

That goat was sailing in a boat,
He was wearing his waterproof coat,
The name of the boat was 'Silly Sally'
And the price nearly everybody thought was doolally.

Robert Stuart Lilley (11)
Ettington Primary School

Once Upon A Rhyme

Once upon a rhyme

In a far and distant time,
Fairy tales, magic and myth were all mine.
I dreamed of adventures with knights of old,
Of giants and dwarfs and heroes so bold,
Of elves and pixies, unicorns too,
And of all the wonderful things I could do,
Of dragons and monsters that roam in the night,
Of many great battles in which I could fight.
I dreamed all the dreams that boys often do
I read all the stories, poetry too.

But now that I'm older and dreams fly away,
Minute by minute and day by day,
I hope somewhere in a distant time,
My own son may remember, 'once upon a rhyme'.

Jack Waller (11)
Ettington Primary School

Fairy Tales

Fairy tales are lovely,
Some of the animals sound really cuddly,
Many of them are quite mad,
Others make you feel sad.

The evil fairy is really glad,
When she is horribly bad.
On the other hand Snow White is the best,
She likes looking at birds in the nest.

So this is the end of my magical poem,
I hope you enjoyed it,
Bye-bye for now.

Did you say 'Wow?'

Bethan Payne (9)
Ettington Primary School

Once Upon A Rhyme

The beauty of the trees,
the softness of the air,
the smell of the grass,
speaks to me.

The top of the mountain,
the thunder of the sky,
the rhythm of the sea,
speaks to me.

The faint look of the stars,
the freshness of the morning,
the snowdrop on the flower,
speaks to me.

The night of fire,
the smell of salmon,
the trail of the sun
and the life that never runs away,
speaks to me.

Charlotte Holmes (9)
Ettington Primary School

The Fairies

The fairies are tiny things,
and they have tiny wings.
Good fairies like people,
bad fairies have destroyed the steeple.
Fairies like small things,
and they wear tiny rings.
I love fairies, what about you?
Sometimes I wonder what they can do.

Jasmine Faulkner-Gant (9)
Ettington Primary School

Floppsy Bunny

Floppsy Bunny is my name
I like to play out in the rain
I play games in the park

Down the slide, here I go
Hope I don't hurt my toe
Whizzing round on the roundabout
Feeling dizzy, what shall I do?

On the swing I fly up high
I almost touch the sky
The sun is orange like a ball
See if I can catch it with my paw.

I am feeling sleepy
Let's go home to bed
Goodnight sleepyhead.

Rosie Sheppard (8)
Ettington Primary School

Space

In my rocket
Flying to the moon
Past the stars
Near Pluto and Mars
Bright lights are flashing
Is someone there?

'Hello Earthling
It's very rude to stare!
Welcome to our planet
Come in if you dare!'

Then the alien gave me a pear
Suddenly I woke up with stardust in my hair!

Bradley Sheppard (10)
Ettington Primary School

Once Upon A Rhyme

Dragons red, dragons green,
Some of them are very mean.

Fairies white, fairies blue,
Some of them are very new.

Goblins black, goblins weird,
Some of them with a long white beard.

Witches evil, witches good,
As I stay under a large hood!

Ben Faulkner-Gant (11)
Ettington Primary School

On My Way To School

On my way to school I saw a man with a bowler hat
It was an old man with a bowler hat
It was an ugly, old man with a bowler hat
It was a tall, ugly, old man with a bowler hat
It was a skinny, tall, ugly, old man with a bowler hat
It was a posh, skinny, tall, ugly, old man with a bowler hat
And he asked me out for tea.

Jack Blackman (9)
Great Alne Primary School

The Trouble With Emily!

The trouble with my friend Emily
Is that she loves to wear your coat,
She mostly sings like a screeching cat,
And pretends she's in a boat!

Once she climbed up on the telly,
And screamed, 'Wow, look at me!'
She put a toad in the fridge,
And jumped right in the tea!

She ran down the corridor,
And thought that she would die!
So jumped down the stairs,
To see if she could fly!

The trouble with my friend Emily,
Is that she's a real pain,
But I wouldn't trade her for anything,
Not even my own plane!

Scarlett Madge (11)
Great Alne Primary School

On My Way To School

On my way to school I saw a car.
It was a big car.
It was a silver, big car.
It was a silver, big, fast car.
It was a bright, silver, big, fast car.
It was a sporty, bright, silver, big, fast car
And it nearly ran me over!

Holly Varnish (9)
Great Alne Primary School

New Teachers

When you find out your old teacher's leaving
You dread to think what kind of things your new teacher
                                    will be thinking.
What kind of thing will she or he do?
I bet she'll do nothing like the old teacher knew.

But when she arrived she seemed alright.
In fact she was great!
She did things her own way,
But boy, were those things better than the old teacher's rules,
That she always used to say!

Sarah Miriam Burch (11)
Great Alne Primary School

Lessons

In our numeracy lesson,
I had a confession,
I did not know what to do,
So I was playing with my shoe.
The teacher was drinking her tea,
I thought she would not notice me,
But she did.
It was like shutting me in a jar with a lid.
I could not hide
I could have died
But just spent five minutes of my playtime in.

Alex Horgan (10)
Great Alne Primary School

The Trouble With My Baby Brother Is . . .

The trouble with my baby brother is,
he always pulls my hair,
he rips my clothes all the time
and shouts, 'It's not fair.'

The trouble with my baby brother is,
he scribbles on my books,
he takes my mirror
just to see how he looks.

The trouble with my baby brother is,
he hits me all the time,
he puts the neighbour's cat in the freezer
and his favourite colour is lime.

The trouble with my baby brother is,
he whines and whines and whines,
he has to get what he wants
or he will shout, 'That's not yours, it's mine!'

Kathryn Major (11)
Great Alne Primary School

The Trouble With My Brother

The trouble with my brother,
He is an awful pain,
He takes up the bathroom
And he blocks up the drain!

The trouble with my brother,
He is very rude.
He comes into my bedroom
And pretends to be a cool dude!

The trouble with my brother,
He dribbles in his sleep.
I've always told him that,
But he just says, 'Beep, beep!'

The trouble with my brother,
He kicks you like mad.
He gets you into trouble
And makes you very sad.

Marianne Piotrowski (11)
Great Alne Primary School

Teacher, Teacher!

Call
> *the*
>> *doctor,*
>>> *call the vet,*
>>>> *I've*
>>> *just*
>> *been*
> *eaten*
>> *by*
>>> *the*
>>>> *teacher's*
>>>>> *pet.*

Jovita West (10)
Great Alne Primary School

Best Friends

Would a best friend . . .
Call you 'Four Eyes'
Talk about you
Say you love someone?
Mine did.

Would a best friend . . .
Blame everything on you
Kick stones at you
Leave you to play on your own?
Mine did.

Would a best friend . . .
Sing a horrible song about you
Shout in your face
Laugh at your haircut?
Mine did.

Would a best friend . . .
Play with you
Have their hair cut like yours
Look you in the eye?
Mine did.

Would a best friend say . . .
'Sorry I said you loved someone'
'Sorry I kicked stones at you'
- 'I thought you'd fallen out with me'?
Mine did.

And would a best friend say, simply,
'Never mind,
That's OK'?
I did.

Jack Dunbar (8)
Great Alne Primary School

Best Friends

Would a best friend . . .
Read your diary
Ignore anything you say
Take your bookmark out of your book?
    Mine did.

Would a best friend . . .
Tell lies about you
Say you love someone
Leave you to play on your own?
    Mine did.

Would a best friend . . .
Rub out your work
Pull funny faces at you
Kick you under the table?
    Mine did.

Would a best friend . . .
Let you read their diary
Play with you all the time
Look you in the eye?
    Mine did.

Would a best friend say . . .
'Sorry I kicked you under the table'
'Sorry I rubbed out your work'
'Sorry I took your bookmark out of your book'
'I thought you'd fallen out with me'?
    Mine did.

And would a best friend simply say,
'Never mind, that's OK'?
    I did.

Rachel Moore (8)
Great Alne Primary School

Best Friends

Would a best friend . . .
Kick stones at you
Ignore you
Hurt you and call you a crybaby?
Mine did.

Would a best friend . . .
Snatch one of your favourite things
Start a rumour about you
Say you love someone?
Mine did.

Would a best friend . . .
Talk about you behind your back
Rub out your work
Stare at you?
Mine did.

Would a best friend . . .
Stop the rumour about you
Write your work for you
Look you in the eye?
Mine did.

Would a best friend say . . .
'Sorry I hurt you and called you a crybaby'
'Sorry I stared at you'
'Sorry I ignored you'
- 'I thought you'd fallen out with me'?
Mine did.

And would a best friend say, simply,
'Never mind,
That's OK'?
I did.

Jacob Turner (7)
Great Alne Primary School

School

School is a lovely place to be,
you can have a giggle and a *hee, hee, hee,*
make new friends each and every day,
the teachers help you every play.
School is a place where you can come to learn.
I sure am grateful I can go to school.

Hannah Smardon (10)
Great Alne Primary School

Cheerful Beach

Watching the white seagulls fly over the glittering sea,
Touching sand as it runs through my fingers,
Listening to the happy people having fun,
Smelling hot burgers as they cook,
Tasting cool ice cream as it slides down my throat.

Watching children paddling in the sea,
Touching rough rock pools,
Listening to horses as they trot along,
Smelling the sharp salt,
Tasting Mum's lovely sandwiches.

I wish I could stay forever!

Emma Proctor (11)
Middlemarch School

Night

I feel lonely and tired, curled up in my bed,
a calm and gentle person enters my room.
A loving and sleepy face appears,
black clothes twinkle as he walks across my bedroom floor.
I sometimes feel scared at night.
Night lives in the glowing moon,
he glides through the starlit sky.

Kelly Cooper (10)
Middlemarch School

Night

I feel sleepy alone in my little bed,
as she steps through the window,
covers my room and kisses my head.
She makes shadows on the wall.
She rattles the windows.
When I wake up in the night it is only the wind.

Rosie Kinder (10)
Middlemarch School

Night

I felt lonely, cold and hurt,
He came into the room and then I heard,
The footsteps of a monster and his purr,
I jumped out of bed and ran to the door.

His big googly eyes glared at me as
I raced towards the door
His large feet raged towards me lifting off the floor,
It was a chase that wouldn't last,
The monster ran, his pace was fast.
If he caught me I knew it would be bed at last.

Mitchell Ward (10)
Middlemarch School

Snowflakes

Snowflakes spinning,
Snowflakes spinning
Round and round till they touch the ground.
The Snow Queen comes in an icy drift.
She dances like a snowflake,
Spinning round and round,
She won't get dizzy.
The last snowflake falls, she disappears.
Now, the ground is covered with a fluffy carpet.
It twinkles in the moonlight.
Now, winter is here.

Mollie Rice (8)
Middlemarch School

The Snow

In winter you get snowflakes spinning
and the fluffy snow twinkling.
The Snow Queen comes out in her
lovely, long, sparkling dress,
she has diamonds on,
her hair is curly and long.
She looks so beautiful!
In winter the winds blows
as the heavy snow falls down.
I love winter, I make snowmen.

Rhian Gemma Moore (8)
Middlemarch School

My Mum

She's a squashy old armchair.
She's a door that always opens.
She's a sly old fox.
She's a wise old owl.
She's a pretty sunflower.
A beautiful singer.
A lovely morning.
A fizzy drink.
A nice mum.

Liam Betteridge (10)
Middlemarch School

The Snow

The snowflakes are spinning.
The Snow Queen dances in the air on the darkest night,
The Snow Queen looks at the snowy land
And in the morning, it has turned to ice.

Steven Sadhara (8)
Middlemarch School

Sir Lancelot, Part IV

From her room she cries her tears,
As the red-cross knight appears
The curse might kill her if she fears,
As lots more knights arrive
As they ride down to Camelot,
Sir Lancelot is in love
But then he finds a lovely dove
For the Lady of Shalott.

Samantha Walker (9)
Middlemarch School

Sir Lancelot, Part IV

'Sir Lancelot, Sir Lancelot,' she cried,
As the mirror cracked from side to side,
'The curse has come upon me,' she sighed
As she ran to her bed and cried,
As she looked down to Camelot.
His shiny armour shone in the sky,
As his climb of the tower had just begun
He had a sword but had no gun,
As he climbed to the Lady of Shalott.

Elizabeth Anne Proctor (10)
Middlemarch School

Sir Lancelot

'Sir Lancelot, Sir Lancelot,' she cried,
As the mirror cracked from side to side.
The silver helmet with feathers on
Gleamed and shone in the sun
As he rode down to Camelot, Sir Lancelot.

The bold and brave knight raced through the prickly thorns,
As he blew his trumpet horn,
The red-crossed knight as he thought to fight,
Down to Camelot.
He climbed the tall, giant tower,
As he did so, he picked a flower.
Prince, Sir Lancelot.

He took her in his arms,
As they both looked out of the window
And gazed across the land at the farms.
'You have come for me,' she cried.
She kissed him and the curse was broken,
The Lady of Shalott
And Lancelot.

They jumped out of the castle window
And shouted with glee.
Sir Lancelot said, 'Will you marry me?'
She said 'Yes,' and the day came with great joy.
They got wed and lived in peace and harmony.

Laura Lapper (10)
Middlemarch School

The Sound Collector

(Based on 'The Sound Collector' by Roger McGough)

'A stranger called this morning,
Dressed all in black and grey,
Put every sound into a bag,
And carried them away.'

The rustling of the leaves,
The zipping of the pencil cases,
The shouting of the teachers,
The children running those races.

The clattering of the lunch trolleys, when you push them,
The hissing of the cooker when you cook,
The squeaking of the chairs,
The swishing of the pages of the book.

The crying of the children,
The rattling of the shutters,
The creaking of the door,
And the sound of my teacher when she mutters,

'A stranger called this morning,
He didn't leave his name,
He left us only silence,
Life will never be the same.'

Jessica Quinn-Dobbins (9)
Our Lady's Catholic Primary School

The Sound Collector

(Based on 'The Sound Collector' by Roger McGough)

'A stranger called this morning
Dressed all in black and grey
Put every sound into a bag
And carried them away.'

The gossiping of the teachers
The scraping of the pencils
The thundering of the drums
The children shouting sums

The swaying of the leaves
The screeching of the lunch trolley
The flapping of the pages in the dictionary
The thumping of the balls in PE

The zipping of the pencil cases
The sucking of the milk
The crunching of the crisps
The chomping of the chocolate

The laughter of the playground
The scratching of the matchbox
The clanging of the bell
The tapping of the keyboard

'A stranger called this morning
He didn't leave his name
Left us only silence
Life will never be the same.'

Charlie Jayne Stanley (10)
Our Lady's Catholic Primary School

Sound Collector

(Based on 'The Sound Collector' by Roger McGough)

'A stranger called this morning,
Dressed all in black and grey
Put every sound into a bag
And carried them away.'

The uttering of the children
The ringing of the bell
The talking of the teachers
As they're trying to tell.

The clicking of the keyboard
The zipping of the pencil case
The laughter of the playground
As they're playing kiss chase.

The whispering of the pages
The whistling of the pen
The discussion of reception
As they count to ten.

The scraping of the matchbox
As we say our prayers
The headmistress telling children off
Because their maths book tears.

The clattering of the lunch trolley
The squeaking of the gate
The praying of the children
As they pray to God and saints.

'A stranger called this morning
He didn't leave his name
He left us only silence
Life will never be the same.'

Shannon Hall (10)
Our Lady's Catholic Primary School

The Sound Collector

(Based on 'The Sound Collector' by Roger McGough)

'A stranger called this morning,
Dressed all in black and grey.
Put every sound into a bag,
And carried them away.'

The rustling of the leaves,
The ringing of the bell.
The whining of the children,
As they cry and tell.

The shouting of the teachers,
Making the children hear what they say.
The screaming of the children,
At the end of the day.

The crunching of the crisps,
The rattling of the lunch trolley.
The slurping sounds from the receptions,
Eating their lollies.

The scratching of the pens,
The whispering of the pages.
The ticking of the clock,
Going on for ages.

The stamping of the feet,
The laughter of the playground.
The squealing of the children,
Running round and round.

'A stranger called this morning,
He didn't leave his name.
Left us only silence,
Life will never be the same.'

Rachel Hendry (10)
Our Lady's Catholic Primary School

The Sound Collector

(Based on 'The Sound Collector' by Roger McGough)

'A stranger called this morning
Dressed all in black and grey
Put every sound into a bag
And carried them away.'

The shouting of the teachers
The thumping of the drums
The clapping of the hands
The tapping of the thumbs

The whizzing of the floppy discs
The whirling of the printer
The buzzing of the metal detector
The silence of the winter

'A stranger called this morning
He didn't leave his name
Left us only silence,
Life will never be the same.'

Anthony Kendall (10)
Our Lady's Catholic Primary School

The Sound Collector

(Based on 'The Sound Collector' by Roger McGough)

'A stranger called this morning,
Dressed all in black and grey,'
All the noisy sounds in the school,
He took them right away.

The stamping of the feet,
The zipping of the pencil cases,
The musicians' musical beat,
The whooshing of the shoelaces.

The crunching of the crisps,
The ringing of the doorbell,
The munching of the chips,
As the teacher starts to yell.

'A stranger called this morning,
He didn't leave his name,
Left us only silence,
Life will never be the same.'

Samantha Preece (10)
Our Lady's Catholic Primary School

The Sound Collector

(Based on 'The Sound Collector' by Roger McGough)

'A stranger called this morning
Dressed all in black and grey
Put every sound into a bag
And carried them away.'

The flickering of the lights
Scraping of the matchbox
The creaking of the door
Howling of the fox

The banging of the builders
Clanging of the dinner tray
The screaming of the children
Ringing of the bell at the end of play

'A stranger called this morning
He didn't leave his name
Left us only silence
Life will never be the same.'

James Dyer (9)
Our Lady's Catholic Primary School

The Sound Collector

(Based on 'The Sound Collector' by Roger McGough)

'A stranger called this morning,
Dressed in black and grey,
Put every sound into a bag,
And carried them away.'

The calling of your friends,
The crying of children for their mums,
The squeaking of the gate
And the banging of the drums.

The flushing of the toilet,
The dripping of the tap,
The talking of the teacher
And the children playing with a map

The clattering of the lunch trolley
The ringing of the bell,
The clicking of the keyboard,
The whispers of the children as their tales they tell.

'A stranger called this morning,
He didn't leave his name,
Left us only silence,
Life will never be the same.'

Daisy Ann Gisbourne (10)
Our Lady's Catholic Primary School

The Sound Collector

(Based on 'The Sound Collector' by Roger McGough)

*'A stranger called this morning
Dressed all in black and grey
Put every sound into a bag
And carried them away.'*

The laughter in the playground
The squeaking of the door
The rustling of the leaves
And the children begging on the floor

The whistling of the whiteboard
The zipping of the pencil cases
The snipping of the scissors
And the children tying laces

The scratching of the matchbox
The scraping of the chair
The twisting of the taps
And the swishing of the girls' hair

*'A stranger called this morning
He didn't leave his name
Left us only silence
Life will never be the same.'*

Christian Hall (10)
Our Lady's Catholic Primary School

The Sound Collector
(Based on 'The Sound Collector' by Roger McGough)

'A stranger called this morning
Dressed all in black and grey
Put every sound into a bag
And carried them away.'

The crunching of the crisps
And the stamping of the feet
The crumbling of the chocolate
Listen to the beat.

The talking of the teachers
Clicking of the keyboard
The laughter of the playground
The swishing of the cord.

The clattering of the lunch trolley
Zipping of the pencil cases
The dripping of the taps and
Win, win, win those races!

'A stranger called this morning
He didn't leave his name
Left us only silence
Life will never be the same.'

Amy Rose Bingham (10)
Our Lady's Catholic Primary School

Quarantine Rap

Quarantine, quarantine,
Everybody's in quarantine
Choppers, boxes, everything!

Quarantine, quarantine,
Clap your hands for quarantine,
There's three weeks to spare,
And everybody's brushing their hair!

Quarantine, quarantine,
Keep on clapping,
Keep on jumping,
For it's the quarantine rap!

Yeah!

Lucie Jade Watson (10)
Our Lady's Catholic Primary School

My Hamster

Happy, delightful little creature.
Cute, soft, furry and sweet, they are her features,
With little ears and tiny whiskers.
She runs around so much,
I'm surprised she doesn't get blisters.
She has beady eyes that follow you around the room.
In the night she looks up at the moon.
Gnawing at her bars,
She looks like she could kill.

Her name is Phil.

Tessa Smallbone (11)
Our Lady's Catholic Primary School

Lizzy Who Played Tricks And Met Her Match

There once was a girl called Lizzy
She was walking down the street with something fizzy
Her life was a complete and utter bore
So she decided to knock on someone's door.

Her mother always said to her,
'Don't you dare!'
But little Lizzy didn't care
She knocked on the door
Then she saw
An old lady with a mallet.

She clobbered Lizzy on the head
Crash!
Bang!
Wallop!

She was dead . . .

Emily Atherton (10)
Our Lady's Catholic Primary School

Pam, Who Ran Away

There was a girl whose name was Pam
She had a boyfriend whose name was Sam
Every day they saw each other
They even agreed it with their mothers.

One day they ran away,
Only to the railway
Pam decided to sit on the track
But suddenly she fell on her back.

Sam ran up to the first-aid box
And quickly got eaten by a fox
Pam got run over by the train
And so their mothers went insane!

Danielle Kessey (11)
Our Lady's Catholic Primary School

I Am . . .

I am a butterfly, I'm beautiful and colourful.
I am a rose, I'm prickly and scented.
I'm a bed, I'm sleepy and lazy and restful and comfy.
I am an Audi, I'm fast, luxurious and sporty.
I am the colour pale pink,
I'm pretty and pale and soft and gentle and smooth.
I am chocolate, I'm bubbly and shiny.
I am a pair of shoes, I'm squeaky and old and tatty.
I am the Empire State Building, I'm tall and stately and elegant
And enormous.

Jenny Roberts (10)
Our Lady's Catholic Primary School

Ray, The Greedy Dog

People say one day
There was a greedy dog called Ray
He saw a butcher's bone
In the background he heard a phone
The butcher left the bone
Then Ray nabbed the bone
And ran away from the phone.

He was ready for his meal
But this was his Achilles heel . . .
He was so greedy
He ate it too speedily

It got stuck on the way
And it wouldn't go away
He's still got it to this day.

Rory Kavanagh (10)
Our Lady's Catholic Primary School

I Am . . .

I am a monkey, active and cheeky.
I am a sunflower, tall and yellow.
I am a motorbike, fast and quick.
I am a carrot, thin and healthy.
I am a scarf, thin and long.
I am a Twin Tower, thin and tall.
I am a fire, tough and strong.
I am a trumpet, loud and shouting.

Chloe Shaw (11)
Our Lady's Catholic Primary School

Tommy, Who Swam In The Sea
And Was Swept Away

Poor old Tommy, he was on holiday
On a tropical island called Malubay.
He was staying with his family
On the coast next to the sea.

On his last day the sea was wild
The sun was cool, the wind was mild.
In he jumped and played away
He did not know it was his last day!

The sea swept him out away from the shore
He knew he wouldn't live; he would die for sure.
So it happened on holiday
On a tropical island called Malubay.

Michael Bennett (10)
Our Lady's Catholic Primary School

Jim, Who Went Swimming In The Sea
And Was Never Seen Again

There was a boy whose name was Jim
All his friends admired him
He went swimming in the sea
Every day since he was three
But one day a red flag flew
Above the sea, greeny-blue.

He was still going to go
Even though his friends said, *'No!'*
He didn't pay any heed to them
And was never seen again.
His mum and dad, they were distraught,
Because Jim swam before he thought.

Arthur Bennett (10)
Our Lady's Catholic Primary School

The Witches

The witches are mean witches,
They destroy football pitches,
They fly up to the sky,
They have green spots
And loads of dots,
They have blue or green skin,
They are very thin,
They eat frogs, yuck!
They have legs that get stuck,
You don't want to meet them or you might be dead,
You won't get fed,
You know what is said,
If you are lucky you might get bread,
They wear hats,
They have pet rats,
I think I might try to fly up to the sky,
On a broomstick,
I might be sick!

Amelia Hopkins (9)
St Faith's CE Junior School, Alcester

Flowers

F resh, red, white and yellow roses,
L ilacs, lilies with green stems,
O rchids in a pink pot,
W e hate weeds,
E verlasting turquoise leaves,
R ed and blue pansies,
S ilver sunflowers glitter in the light
as they love the sun.

Charlotte Howl (10)
St Faith's CE Junior School, Alcester

Spring

S pring clouds go flying by
P ink blossoms grow with pride
R ed and brown trees grow bright green leaves
I n spring all flowers grow
N ow it's autumn when all leaves are dead
G o back to spring because all leaves are red.

Jack Miles (10)
St Faith's CE Junior School, Alcester

Watch The Snow Fall

Watch the snow fall,
It sticks on walls,
Watch the ground go white,
Look at the sight,
Cold wind blows,
The sun goes.

Out children go,
Playing with the snow,
Snowballs flying around,
The big gong sounds,
Back in they go,
People say, 'No!'
The sun comes out,
The snow melts,
And that is the poem of
'Watch the snow fall'.

Adam Woollacott (10)
St Faith's CE Junior School, Alcester

Keep Out!

Treasure is bright and gold,
Whoever has it will be bold.
Treasure will make you wealthy,
But you won't be healthy.
If you find it, you will be cursed,
Because I was the first.

Matthew Laight (10)
St Faith's CE Junior School, Alcester

The Leopard

The leopard, patched black in the grass
Its presence, unaware to others.

Sneaking like a spy past a camera
Then a bullet, prey-bound
Then silence, like the stars at night -
The prey is dead.

The carcass, blood-red, dragged up a shady tree
A munchy, meaty meal to be had
Tomorrow's another day.

Ben Smith (11)
St Faith's CE Junior School, Alcester

Krat Dragon

K rat dragons are mean,
R ipping off flesh,
A rms are bleeding,
T ears make a mess.

D rooling the blood,
R ipping off flesh,
A rms are bleeding,
G ory it is.
O ranges make them weaker.
N oise they make.

Chris Hodge (10)
St Faith's CE Junior School, Alcester

Maths

Maths is so boring
I'm always, always snoring
My teacher goes on
About sums that are wrong
I get sums wrong
Because my mind just goes *bong!*

Every day is the same,
Sometimes I think my class is so lame
Maths is so stupid
Just the same as Cupid.

The work is so hard
Making a card isn't so hard.

Can't we just do that instead?

Lucy Sloan (9)
St Faith's CE Junior School, Alcester

Snowman

S am the
N oble
O range, hot snowman
W atering every second, but
M anaging to stay
A live in the
N ew temperature. Getting hotter all the time.

Eleanor Reeves (9)
St Faith's CE Junior School, Alcester

Sniper

S ilent as a breeze
N asty piercing bullets
I nvisible to the human eye
P ulverising people as it goes
E vaporating humankind
R angers cloaked in the distance.

Jamie Glenn (10)
St Faith's CE Junior School, Alcester

Stratford School

At Stratford School,
There is a large pool.
The maths is boring,
Everyone is snoring,
No one is writing,
Everyone is fighting.
The head teacher's in bed,
Cuddling his bear Ted,
Because there's a little child,
Who's absolutely wild.
The children play,
The teachers pray they stay out all day.
Then the kids come in,
And put the teachers in bins.
In come the boys,
Throwing toys.
In come the girls,
Nicking the teacher's pearls.
And that's the story
Of Stratford School.

Sean Blyth (9)
St Faith's CE Junior School, Alcester

Winter's Morning

My perfect winter's morning would have . . .
A clear, pale blue sky,
The icy, chilly breeze would blow in my face,
And the sunlight would give me warmth.
The ground would be shiny and glistening through my eyes.
Clear crystals, I would imagine on the ground
Reflecting in the sunlight.
Cobwebs glistening in the mist.
All the colours, I could see in the sky would be
Pale orange, pink, grey and blue.
That would be my perfect winter's morning.

Mae Yee Chek (10)
St Faith's CE Junior School, Alcester

Classroom

T he classroom is a mess,
H ats and gloves everywhere,
E lephants trampling on the desk,

C ucumbers on their heads,
L ucy listing spellings ready for the test,
'A little
S now,'
S aid Shannon,
R oaming round the room,
O utside all white,
O h what a sight,
M y mum will need a broom!

Samantha Richards (10)
St Faith's CE Junior School, Alcester

Snowflake

Small confetti,
Twirling and twirling,
Down towards the ground.

They emerge from grey sky,
Like silken silver,
Twisting round and round.

They flutter through the air,
With a cushion to catch them,
Snowflakes don't make a sound.

Sophie Bird (10)
St Faith's CE Junior School, Alcester

Dolphins

As I walked around the corner,
I heard a noise,
It wasn't any ordinary noise
It was a clicking, chattering noise
I looked towards it and it was the most
Beautiful thing that I had ever heard

It was a pink dolphin.
I thought the dolphin was a pink submarine,
As it moved, it slowly changed colour,
It looked like mermaids' scales.

I rubbed my eyes,
It couldn't be true,
I pinched myself to find time had marched on.

I saw a red mark on my arm like a burn,
It reminded me of my dream.

Charlotte Maycock (10)
St Faith's CE Junior School, Alcester

The Mountain

Snow of glistening white,
Shining in the sun
Falling like a silken feather.

Deadly footprints
Spoil the white glisten of the ground.

The mountain like an arched back
Ready to fall.

Mounds like lollipops
Walking everywhere.

Katie Hand (11)
St Faith's CE Junior School, Alcester

Leopard

Stalking oblivious prey,
Wildebeest, gazelle,
Cunning, yet careful,
A bullet when chasing,
Stealthily sniffing the air,
Her cubs obediently follow,
Hanging like a vine from trees,
Curious cubs, cautious mum,
Protective like my mother.

Patrick Sarson (10)
St Faith's CE Junior School, Alcester

Make-Believe

Make-believe when dead, come back alive
Make-believe a tooth as big as a roof
Make-believe a snail as big as a whale
Make-believe a duck as big as a truck
Make-believe a spider as big as a bottle of cider
Make-believe a chair as big as a bear
Make-believe a sock as big as a clock
Make-believe a mouse as big as a house
Make-believe a head as big as a bed
Make-believe a beer as big as a pier
Make-believe a tub as big as a pub
Make-believe a bun as big as the sun.

Peter Bridgeford (9)
St Faith's CE Junior School, Alcester

Autumn

Leaves are falling to the ground
as I am playing around.
When I have to go to bed
all the leaves turn red.
Spicy browns and oranges gleam
but in the spring the trees turn green.

April Hands (9)
St Faith's CE Junior School, Alcester

Snow

Snow is drifting slowly down
White snow is crunchy
Children playing in the snow
Playing snowball fights
Throwing cold snowballs
Playing with the white freezing snow.
Then later, let it go!

Katie Hoskins (10)
St Faith's CE Junior School, Alcester

Astronomy

Astronauts blasted in the depths of space
Sun scorching hot, stars in a race
Turning into the blackness, planets orbit and spin
Running around in the dark and dim.
On Earth the people wait
Near the launching pad gate
On TV the crew is intense
Mission Control is very tense
Yet the support they give is very safe.

Joseph Rawlings (9)
St Faith's CE Junior School, Alcester

The Tulip

What's this coming up from the ground?
Making her way through mud and damp
Springing out in a beautiful colour
Purple, my favourite.

The poor tulip pushing her head through tough mud
Springing out her grassy, green body
Standing as still as a statue while the grass heals around her
Waiting.

What's this?
She's opening her inner-self to make the real beauty rise
Wow, what a sight!

Oh look!
What's this?
Millions of tulips awakening
Now there is no grass, just a multicoloured field.

Ellie O'Shea (10)
St Faith's CE Junior School, Alcester

The Sphinx

Picturesque woman head
Lion behind
Sitting on a pillar
Like a pharaoh in bed

Tourists swarm to her
Her riddles, unique
A never-ending question
She has fur

Do not disturb her you little minx
A hunter waiting for her prey
The sand bows down to her
She is a sphinx.

Lauren Matheson (10)
St Faith's CE Junior School, Alcester

The Dragon

Dragon, so shiny-scaled and deadly
Dragon, so black-hearted and evil
Dragon hissing loudly sounding snake-like
Dragon moving secretively
Dragon on his way to kill
Dragon spots his prey and hearts will be broken

Deadly as an adder's strike
Evil as demonic powers
Hissing venom from the mouth of Hell
Moving, subtle, devious, crafty
Predator, avenger, devouring, beast
Focusing, homing, death dealing . . .

Laura Morris (11)
St Faith's CE Junior School, Alcester

School Lunches

S melly sausage,
C old carrots,
H ot dogs,
O ld orange juice,
O dd-shaped oranges,
L emon jelly,

L lama spit,
U ncooked cabbage,
N uggets that are burnt,
C old chips,
H orrible eggs,
E ggshells,
S chool lunches - *yuck!*

Penny Sreeves (9)
St Faith's CE Junior School, Alcester

Witches' Troubles

There were three witches, mad were they.
They ate frogs' legs and chewed dogs' heads.
Gnawed rats' feet and chewed their teeth.

They were really bad, really evil.
They almost got caught for blowing up a fort,
But we never knew they could go to court.

In the end they got away, but with a slight disarray.

The witches were bad, as bad as they could get,
But they still weren't as bad as Jango Fett.

They walked around in fine dresses,
Cursing at the morning presses.

They were so stupid, so mad,
They were the meanest people around,
And you would never guess they were related to Cupid!

Jamie Done (10)
St Faith's CE Junior School, Alcester

Snakes Are . . .

Snakes are cool,
Snakes are slimy,
They come in different shapes and sizes,
Snakes slide across the floor,
And out of the door,
Now there's no more.

Eloise Bonehill (10)
St Faith's CE Junior School, Alcester

Travelling Round The World

Travelling
Travelling round
Travelling round the
Travelling round the world
The world
The world
I've got rickets
I've got to eat crickets
The captain's got the lurgy
The cook's got scurvy
Our sailors died
All their wives cried
Their kids laughed
Because they were daft
Travelling round the world
The world
The world
The world
I'm scared, help, help!
I'm seasick
Give me fruit
Or I'll shoot
It's not safe
The captain's got the lurgy.

Jared Wigmore (9)
St Francis RC Primary School, Bedworth

Travelling Round The World

Travelling round the world
It's such a small boat
Eating rats
Sleeping on hammocks
What shall I do?

Travelling round the world
How much longer?
I am bored
I am hungry
I just want to go home.

Travelling round the world
No fruit
No food
This is not fair
Why can't someone else be here?

Travelling round the world
Over the sea
Up and down
I am all over the place
Travelling round the world.

Kerry Louise O'Connor (9)
St Francis RC Primary School, Bedworth

Travelling Round The World

Travelling round the world
This food is vile
Travelling round the world
We have gone for miles

Travelling round the world
Our water's turned yellow and green
Travelling round the world
That's nothing compared to what I've seen

Travelling round the world
I've got scurvy
Travelling round the world
It's like the lurgy

Travelling round the world
Man overboard
Travelling round the world
Get out the swords

Travelling round the world
Help, I am scared
Travelling round the world
Like you cared!

Travelling round the world
I feel drowsy
Travelling round the world
You're lousy.

Laura Wilthew (10)
St Francis RC Primary School, Bedworth

Travelling Round The World

Travelling round the world,
Eating a rat,
Making us fat,
Look at my hat,
Travelling round the world.

Travelling round the world,
Help I've got scurvy!
Help, I've got scurvy!
Help, I've got scurvy!
Travelling round the world.

Travelling round the world,
Sleeping in hammocks with a rat in my hat,
Have you seen that rat?
He's in my hat,
Travelling round the world.

Travelling round the world,
All hands on deck,
Aaaarrrggghhh! The net,
Oh what the heck,
Travelling round the world.

Travelling round the world,
I'm tired,
You're fired,
I'm hired,
Travelling round the world.

Travelling round the world,
This water's green,
It looks quite mean,
It's not clean,
Travelling round the world.

Sarah Atkins (10)
St Francis RC Primary School, Bedworth

Travelling Round The World

I want to go home, home, home
Home, home, I can't help having a moan.

Travelling round the world,
I want proper food
Can you stop having a mood?
I can't help having a moan,
I want proper food
And can you stop being in a moan?
Travelling round the world.

I want proper food,
And can you stop having a mood?

The water's green,
Isn't the captain mean?

Travelling round the world.

Where's the fruit?
Argh!
There's a rat in my boot,
Scurvy, scurvy, scurvy!
Travelling round the world.

I feel seasick I need something to lick.
This food is vile
How many more miles till we get there?
Travelling round the world.

Roseanne Howard (9)
St Francis RC Primary School, Bedworth

Travelling Round The World

One day Magellan went off with men,
And in one month off went ten,
Travelling round the world,
'Land ahoy,' yelled a man called Ben,
Travelling round the world.

For winter in America they'd reach,
And spent several months on the beach,
Travelling round the world,
To the Americans about Jesus they'd teach,
Travelling round the world.

Pacific Ocean they had to cross,
They were getting quite bored of their Spanish boss,
Travelling round the world,
Thanks to scurvy there was a massive loss,
Travelling round the world.

In Asia, they had a great war,
But their fighting skills were very poor,
Travelling round the world,
Their Asian spears could really sour,
Travelling round the world.

Tanks to the Philippines, Magellan died,
No one like him, no one cried.
Travelling round the world,
Next came the Atlantic Ocean deep and wide.

Portuguese attacked again, again,
Causing the men death and pain,
Travelling round the world,
At last 18 men got back to Spain,
Victoria made it round the world.

Scott Harris (9)
St Francis RC Primary School, Bedworth

Travelling Round The World

Travelling around the world
The world, the world
Travelling around the world
The world, the world
Travelling around the world

The food's vile
It's not my fault, I didn't know it was longer than a mile
I've got scurvy, I've got rickets
Oh no, I'm missing the cricket!
Travelling around the world

Will you stop snoring?
It's really boring
It's not my fault
I need one bolt
Travelling around the world

Travelling around the world
The world, the world
Travelling around the world
The world, the world
Travelling around the world

How much longer?
I'm going 'conga bonga'
Man overboard
Oh help me Lord
Travelling around the world

Travelling around the world
The world, the world,
Travelling around the world
The world, the world
Travelling around the world.

Arandeep Hayer (9)
St Francis RC Primary School, Bedworth

Travelling Round The World

Travelling around the world
Magellan died, not of scurvy, not of rickets
Only spears, swords and dry biscuits
Travelling around the world.

Travelling around the world
In a 75-foot ship.
Eating no fruit hurts my feet
Travelling around the world.

Travelling around the world
I have the lurgy
My mate has got scurvy
Travelling around the world.

Travelling around the world
Man overboard
I am really bored
Travelling around the world.

Michael McDade (10)
St Francis RC Primary School, Bedworth

Travelling Round The World

Travelling
Travelling round
Travelling round the
Travelling round the world I go
You can travel in a car, or you can travel in a plane, train or a boat,
Which do you want to travel in? Because I chose to travel in a plane
Because it goes up high so I am not shy to travel in a plane.
It is not very plain because they're first class and second class.
It is good to travel in a plane because you get to see the sky.
It isn't shy, it has got clouds and the sun, which looks like a
yellow bun.

Joseph Dell (9)
St Francis RC Primary School, Bedworth

Around The World

Travelling around the world in a plane,
    meeting people on the train.
        Travelling around the world I go,
            blooming heck! This ship is slow.
                Sometimes I think I'm going to die,
                    but then I'm saved by apple pie.
                        Travelling over stormy seas,
                            people growing up to my knees.

Ryan Michael Keane (10)
St Francis RC Primary School, Bedworth

Travelling Round The World

I am travelling the world
I feel sick
I feel drowsy, drowsy
I want to go home
I want proper food
I feel sleepy
I want some rum
Please load the guns
Beautiful, I want a bun
All hands on deck
I think I've got scurvy.

Daniel Smith-Walker (9)
St Francis RC Primary School, Bedworth

Travelling Round The World

The ship, the ship wants rum
But we have none,
Go back to the hammock, yes, yes, yes
No, no, no, you can't make me do anything
Rats get them, let's go back into the hammock
No, no, no, I think so, yes, yes, I will
Can't make me do everything, OK, no
I want rum, there is no one overboard.

Steven Haddon (9)
St Francis RC Primary School, Bedworth

Travelling Round The World

Travelling round the world
The world, the world,
Travelling round the world
The world, the world
Travelling round the whole wide world

I'm seasick,
I think I see a tick,
All hands on deck,
Oh, what the heck,
Travelling round the world

A sailor's died,
Quick, let's hide,
I have rickets,
Be quiet, you silly crickets
Travelling round the world

I've got scurvy,
This barrel's very curvy,
Stop snoring,
It's a bit boring,
Travelling round the world

Man overboard,
This wood's been sawed,
Look at the rum,
It makes you want to hum
Travelling round the world

Travelling round the world
The world, the world
Travelling round the world
The world, the world
Travelling round the whole wide world.

Jessica Neale (9)
St Francis RC Primary School, Bedworth

Travelling Round The World

While travelling around the world
Sailors ate rats, sailors ate sawdust
Sailors ate mouldy food but
No fruit and only drank yellowish water.

While travelling around the world
The sailors were in a line, a line
For the hammocks and one
Told another, 'I'm tired, I'm tired.'

Travelling around the world
It became winter
But a man got a splinter
Men became cold
And the ship wouldn't hold.

Travelling around the ocean
We all got seasick emotion
I want to go home
Because I'm all alone.

Man overboard, the water is deep
But I just want to go to sleep
Help! Help! Oh why don't you shout for an anchor?

While travelling round the world
Sailors said, 'Are we home yet? Are we home yet?'
Just as we got home, a man shouted,
    'Land ahoy!'

Sophie Neale (9)
St Francis RC Primary School, Bedworth

Travelling Round The World

Travelling round the world,
Through the sun and rain,
On a boat or on a plane,
Travelling round the world.

Travelling round the world,
Through the night and day,
Watching all the dolphins play,
Travelling round the world.

Travelling round the world,
Seeing all new people,
Who are very grateful,
Travelling round the world.

Travelling round the world,
From one country to another,
With people who need a mother,
Travelling round the world.

Travelling round the world,
That's where I go,
Sending things to people I know,
Travelling round the world.

Travelling round the world,
Going places where I haven't seen,
With nice houses that are clean,
Travelling round the world.

Travelling round the world,
Seeing people rich and famous,
I met someone called Seamus,
Travelling round the world,

I travelled round the world,
So now you've gone too.

Laura James (10)
St Francis RC Primary School, Bedworth

Travelling Round The World

Travelling round the world,
I sleep in a hammock all curled,
Eating rats and seeing bats,
Travelling round the world.

The water, yellow and green,
What a sight I'd seen,
Travelling round the world,
Mouldy food, what a mood,
Travelling round the world.

I want to go home,
All I do is sit and moan,
Travelling round the world,
'No fruit,' the captain said,
'You little brute.'

Travelling round the world,
My friend has rickets,
I said, 'I saw some crickets,'
Travelling round the world,
Travelling round the world.

Where are we, what do you see?
The food is vile,
It is just a mile,
Travelling round the world,
I meet a man curled.

Travelling round the world,
Travelling round the world,
Travelling, travelling, travelling.
Round, round, round
The world, the world, the world.

Charlotte Burkinshaw (10)
St Francis RC Primary School, Bedworth

Travelling Round The World

Travelling round the world, with our big happy crew.
Travelling round the world, we're in a hurry.
Travelling round the world, fancy a curry.
Travelling round the world, me mate's got rickets.
Oh no, I'm missing the cricket!
Travelling round the world I go.

James Ingleston (9)
St Francis RC Primary School, Bedworth

Round The World

I am a little leprechaun.
I go from country to country
To collect my corn.
I said to myself, *I've got to get gold.*
That's what I was told.
The world is so big,
I said, 'I'll eat that pig
So I get the jig.'
I travel and travel
Until I get into the gravel.
I said, 'This is great,
But I'm going to faint.'

Ross O' Donoghue (9)
St Francis RC Primary School, Bedworth

Travelling Round The World

Travelling round the world I see
Dolphins jumping up at me
I'm travelling on a tiny ship
Then I give my crew a tip

People walk and talk to me
Then they ask me for tea
People say, 'Hello' and 'Bye'
Then I feel I'm going to die

The sunset is so pretty
Oh my little kitty
It's a pity he's gone today
Then people say, 'Hey.'

Then it comes to Christmas time
Then we put out the food and wine
Then stockings are put up in a line
So we go downstairs and open them.

Lucinda Batchelor (9)
St Francis RC Primary School, Bedworth

Travelling Round The World

Travelling
Travelling around
Travelling around the
Travelling around the world
The world, the whole wide world

Eating rats, it's better than cats
Stop that Mark, I've just seen a shark
This is boring the rain is pouring

Travelling
Travelling around
Travelling around the
Travelling around the world
The world, the whole wide world

All hands on deck, the birds might peck
It's not safe, I've seen a snake
I've got rickets
I've found some tickets and I'm playing cricket

Travelling
Travelling around
Travelling around the
Travelling around the world
The world, the whole wide world

They're shouting my name, I've seen a plane and a train
I want to go home, I'm on my own
And I've lost my mobile phone.

Thomas Moore (10)
St Francis RC Primary School, Bedworth

Wild Spirit

Every night I creep outside,
When everything is still,
I walk along a shadowy path,
But I always have a chill.

Stumbling past the snowy fields,
An owl soars by to hide,
Then all is calm and all is quiet,
By the tree so old and wide.

What's that in the distance
On the hills so far away?
A wild horse lifts his head,
And then begins to neigh.

Galloping free across the hilltops,
Mane flowing with Earth's song,
His heart throbbing wildly
My spirit jumps along.

Madeleine Glasbey (9)
St Mary's RC Primary School, Studley

My Sausage Dog

My sausage dog is very long,
Once we pushed him in the pond,
The pond is so deep it smells too,
So sometimes we are sick in the loo.

He really is so very soft,
One day he climbed into the loft.
He jumped out covered in dust,
So my mum made such a fuss.

My sausage dog is really slow,
But he looks so pretty when he wears his bow
We really think he's a lovely dog,
So sometimes he sleeps on the garden log.

Grace Lynskey (8)
St Mary's RC Primary School, Studley

My Mad Dog

I have a dog who is very mad,
and sometimes he's very bad,

My mad dog is crazy,
My mad dog is lazy,

My mad dog has a big tummy,
because his food is very yummy,

My dog Alfie is very big,
and likes to play tig,

He dribbles all over the place,
and in my face,

He always goes in the bin,
and takes out a tin,

Every time he jumps in a puddle,
I say, 'Don't come near me
because you won't get a cuddle.'

Even though he's as naughty as can be,
he's still the best dog in the world for me.

Elizabeth Edgar (8)
St Mary's RC Primary School, Studley

Mermaids

In the water, blue and green,
No one knows as they're not seen.
Always deep down and out of sight,
On the ocean floor where there's no light.
Flipping their fins in the sea,
Half fish, half you and me.
Breathing air and breathing water,
Holding close a son or daughter.
Exploring shipwrecks on the seabed,
They might be fearless, they might be scared.
In the water, green and blue,
No one knows what they do!

Rose Allcock (10)
St Nicholas' CE Primary School, Kenilworth

Night Fright!

I woke up suddenly in the night,
I heard something that gave me a fright,
I heard someone creep up the staircase,
It came into my room and had a ghostly white face,
I hid under my covers,
I held them tight,
I really don't like it late at night,
Then I heard a voice say,
'Johnny, are you okay?'
I peeped out to see who was there,
It was my mother with her long, swaying hair,
'I thought you were a monster,' I said,
'Oh, Johnny, drink this water and go back to bed!'

Ella Hall (11)
St Nicholas' CE Primary School, Kenilworth

Leaf Haiku

Dead leaf on the floor
All crispy like a biscuit
Making crackly noise.

Joanne Marshall (10)
St Nicholas' CE Primary School, Kenilworth

Cats

Cats, cats
Jumping around
Cats, cats
They are found:
In the city
In the street
In the garden
By your feet
In the flowerpot
In the shed
Always wanting
To be fed.

Georgina Eastaugh (10)
St Nicholas' CE Primary School, Kenilworth

School Bag

Pens and pencils, bits of fluff
Not really very interesting stuff
But if you look quite carefully
Take some time and you will see . . .

Bugs and beetles, bits of dirt
Last month's English homework
School trip slips and dinner money
A ten-pound note, now that is funny!

Last year's bus pass, old and worn
Your favourite book, all tattered and torn
Old sticky toffee, stuck to the bottom
Overdue library books, almost forgotten!

But if you take out all this treasure
That once upon a time, gave you pleasure
Your school bag will seem so empty and grey
Until you load it up . . . another day!

Isabel Sturt (10)
St Nicholas' CE Primary School, Kenilworth

January Day - Haiku

We see children play
The sun is shining brightly
Our hair is blowing.

Bethany Thorne (9)
St Nicholas' CE Primary School, Kenilworth

Waiting

At a sister's swimming lesson,
Waiting for it to end,
Finished my maths homework,
This drives me round the bend!

Other sister playing 'hangman',
Sky darkening outside,
Swimming teacher shouting,
Getting more bored inside.

Waves rippling in the pool,
Wall light glaring,
I suddenly have to scream,
'Aarrgghhh!'
Everybody staring.

Georgia Sturt (8)
St Nicholas' CE Primary School, Kenilworth

The Playground - Haiku

Out in the playground
In the bitterly cold wind
We stood very still.

Megan Edgington (10)
St Nicholas' CE Primary School, Kenilworth

The Secret Man

When the night is young,
A secret man,
Rides swiftly and silently
Through the dim-lit path.

As the moonlight shines,
It sees two pistols,
With silver handles,
Under the man's scarlet coat.

His face is hidden from view,
'Cause of the shadow from
A French cocked hat
And frilled lace at his chin.

On his feet are
Posh polished boots,
Covering his doe-skinned breeches
Holding a rapier over his thigh.

When the night is young,
He rides swiftly and silently,
Until all signs of night,
Are gone.

Jacob Mansbridge (11)
St Nicholas' CE Primary School, Kenilworth

The High Tree - Haikus

Out upon the field
A sturdy old hairy tree
Like a large tower

Out upon the field
A very large tree grows tall
With twiggy branches

Out upon the field
A small tree can start growing
As the old tree falls.

Ben Moseley (9)
St Nicholas' CE Primary School, Kenilworth

What's Up . . . What's Down?

What's up?   What's down?
The air   The floor
Up from that?   Down from that?
The clouds   The 3rd floor
Up from that?   Down from that?
Aeroplanes   The 2nd floor
Up from that?   Down from that?
The Earth's atmosphere   The 1st floor
Up from that?   Down from that?
Space   Ground floor
Up from that?   Next?
Stars   The Earth's crust
Up from that?   Next?
                              The Earth's core
                              Next ?

It's teatime
'Ow!'   It's breakfast
'Mum, what's up?'   'Dad, what's down?'

Gregory Hulme (10)
St Nicholas' CE Primary School, Kenilworth

Storm - Haiku

Out in the wet storm
Kenilworth town lies all still
No movement at all.

Nathan Wood (11)
St Nicholas' CE Primary School, Kenilworth

Friends

When you're feeling lonely,
All you need are friends.
When you're needing help,
All you need are friends
When your heart stops beating
        Your only friend
                Is God.

Joshua Bonser (10)
St Peter's CE Primary School, Market Bosworth

The Dopey Sailor

There once was an abnormal sailor
Who was well known to be a bit of a failure
He drove a big ship
He had a long kip
And ended up in Australia.

Joe Duckney (10)
St Peter's CE Primary School, Market Bosworth

At The Park

At the park it was windy,
At the park it was cold,
At the park we had fun,
And I had an iced bun.
I went on the swing,
I went on the slide,
Then I went to run and hide.
Oh what a wonderful
                day at the park.

Sophie Lacey (6)
St Peter's CE Primary School, Market Bosworth

The Bunny

A bunny rabbit hopping wild,
Looking for a lonely child,
Then he saw at his door,

An unhappy little girl,
Playing with her dolly's curl,
Then she saw him looking in.

This is when he made a run,
The girl did have so much fun,
Playing here and laughing there.

All the sadness left behind,
Wondering what else they would find,
They stayed together forever and ever.

Oh what a happy bunny rabbit.

Ceri Norton (11)
St Peter's CE Primary School, Market Bosworth

Summer

The bees are being born in summer,
the flowers are not looking glummer,
the sun does shine and the farmer combines
and that is what's born in summer.

Golden rays shoot down from the sun,
much thinner than an iced bun,
flowers are shooting up from the earth,
while baby animals are giving their birth.

Summer is my favourite time,
and now I am saying, 'Goodbye.'

Helena Parkes (7)
St Peter's CE Primary School, Market Bosworth

When Sun Goes Down

When sun goes down,
Mums are wearing gowns,
When sun goes up,
Dads are drinking from cups.
When sun sets,
People aren't going on jets,
When moon goes up,
Dogs don't have pups.
When moon goes down,
Sun comes up.

Callum Denore (7)
St Peter's CE Primary School, Market Bosworth

Guess Who?

Cat chaser
Good racer
Loud barker
House marker
It's extremely fast,
Like a blast.
Very strong,
And so long.

Mahin Kohli (10)
St Peter's CE Primary School, Market Bosworth

The Golden Sunlight

The golden sunlight,
It nearly gave me a fright,
I came home, it was late,
My food was on my plate.

The house was cold,
It had some mould,
I took the dog for a walk,
My mum unscrewed the cork.

I came home for tea,
With my brother Lee.

Lucy Mary Fallon (8)
St Peter's CE Primary School, Market Bosworth

Stars

Stars are shiny in the sky
while the sun is saying goodbye.
The moon is gleaming,
it's coming up now
while all the stars start to bow.
The stars like dancing
so they start to dance
while the moon joins in
and starts to
                prance!

Chloe McDougall (7)
St Peter's CE Primary School, Market Bosworth

Moor Horse

I went to the misty moor.
I saw all the thick fog.
Out of the mist,
I saw a ghostly white figure of a horse.

It had a moonlit mane and tail.
Its body pure white,
More ghost-like than anything.
I looked even closer,

But it was not a horse, it was a ghost!
'Argh! It's a ghost!'

Grace Woolmer (8)
St Peter's CE Primary School, Market Bosworth

Kennings Cat

Tree climber
Purr rhymer
Sofa sleeper
Mouse eater
Night starer
Fish scarer
Midnight prowler
Tiny howler
Rat racer
Dog pacer.

George Bassnett (10)
St Peter's CE Primary School, Market Bosworth

Kennings Cat

Lazy eater
Spider beater
Tree climber
Perfect timer
Loud purrer
Sleep stirrer
High jumper
Fat slumper
Slick runner
Dog stunner.

Hannah Jackson (9)
St Peter's CE Primary School, Market Bosworth

Kennings Playground

Teachers shouting
People playing
Children crying
Kids singing
Balls bouncing
Everyone shouting
People telling
Girls hopping
Everyone running
People misbehaving.

Michael Maguire (10)
St Peter's CE Primary School, Market Bosworth

My Family

My mum, she is quite funny,
She draws and cooks and sews,
She loves to go to the shops,
To spend a lot of money

My dad, he is good fun to know,
He always wants to play,
When he's around we mess about,
He takes us where we want to go

My sister is just like me,
She's pretty, kind and clever,
You cannot tell if I am she,
We are identical twins you see.

The four of us, we make a team,
Our family together,
We love each other very much,
And always will forever.

Lucy Sandford-James (7)
St Peter's CE Primary School, Market Bosworth

Growing Up

When I was very little
About the age of one
I didn't know very much
My life had just begun

When I was a bit bigger
About the age of three
I had learned a few things
I knew that I was me

When I was even older
About the age of six
I'd make people laugh at me
By doing magic tricks

Now I'm nearly eight
I'm getting really clever
I can write and read and count and swim
And won't stop learning ever.

Anna Sandford-James (7)
St Peter's CE Primary School, Market Bosworth

Kennings Best Friend

Secret sharer,
Make-up wearer,
Phone caller,
Skilled netballer,
Text sender,
Clothes lender,
Heavy shopper,
Fashion topper,
Disco dancer,
Great prancer.

Ellie Hicklin (11)
St Peter's CE Primary School, Market Bosworth

Kennings Dad

Hard worker
Greenhouse lurker
Food maker
Rubbish baker
Table layer
Football player
Loud snorer
Annoying borer
Play fighter
Screw tightener.

Sophie Powell (11)
St Peter's CE Primary School, Market Bosworth

Kennings Earthquake

Ground cracker
Tree smacker
Earth shaker
Wave maker
News breaker
People taker
House smasher
Rock basher
Business buster
Metal ruster.

Joseph Rowland (9)
St Peter's CE Primary School, Market Bosworth

Kennings Snake

Bone smasher
Quick lasher
Ground slitherer
Prey quiverer
Venom biter
Angry smiter
Loud rattler
Hard battler
Swift mover
People hoover
Hot bearer
Massive scarer
Lip smacker
Quiet attacker
Fast killer
No spiller.

Mike Titley (10)
St Peter's CE Primary School, Market Bosworth

Kennings Sea

Wave crasher,
Bone basher,
Seagull swimmer,
Rock slimmer,
Sand lover,
Seaweed cover,
People sweeper,
Inflatable keeper,
Boat rider,
Sea diver.

Gemma Steel (10)
St Peter's CE Primary School, Market Bosworth

Rhyme Time

There are food rhymes with fries and a chocolate cake,
There are food rhymes with fries and strawberry milkshake.

There are rhymes of a mole that dug a great hole,
There are rhymes of a mole that liked to eat coal.

There are rhymes of snow that made it blow,
There are rhymes of snow that made quite a show!

There are rhymes of a fall with a cry and a call,
There are rhymes of a fall with a great, big, blue ball.

There are rhymes of this and that,
There are rhymes of a cat.

I now think this rhyme song is perfectly sung,
But I'd like to say once more to everyone . . .

There are rhymes, rhymes, rhymes!

Annabelle Saunders (8)
St Peter's CE Primary School, Market Bosworth

Wild Cats

There are different wild cat types,
patterned with either spots or stripes.
They groom their fur,
while they purr.
They can run very fast,
while the time goes past.
The little cubs learn to swim,
and the lioness has had a cub called Tim.
They go under trees for shade,
while the sun goes down and starts to fade.

Chloe Lockett (10)
St Peter's CE Primary School, Market Bosworth

Kennings Fox

Rabbit snatcher
Bird catcher
Bone breaker
Human hater
Hound fighter
Badger biter
Fast pouncer
Unlikely bouncer
Chicken killer
Stomach filler
Easy tricker
Spiteful licker.

Alex Coney (10)
St Peter's CE Primary School, Market Bosworth

Winter Prayer

I looked up to see the grass glittering like emeralds,
The only thing that had any happiness about it,
The rest of the world was covered in a layer of sadness,
I felt weak and joyless despite it being nearly Christmas,
Looking up at the sky, I began to pray to God for happiness.

It was then I saw it, a giant spider's web coated in ice,
A dark shadow standing proud on the bright green rug
                              full of crispiness,
Its frosty fingers reaching out to save me from the sadness,
Guarding the grass from all the evil and wickedness,
It felt like this magical tree was God's answer to my prayer.

As I stood there lost, looking at the angel in disguise,
All the happiness came quickly rushing back to me,
The moon now looked like a beautiful smiling face in the sky,
The thick layer of evil sadness lifted off the world,
I was over the kindly moon; God had answered my prayer.

Rachel Naylor (11)
St Peter's CE Primary School, Market Bosworth

Teddy Bear

Sweet, kind,
Loving and bright,
Lights up my heart
With all his might.

In the night,
I hug him close,
Of all my toys,
I love him most.

He understands,
When I cry,
I'll keep him with me,
Till I die.

My teddy bear,
Soft and warm,
He comes in,
The best form.

He's mine,
He always will be,
Bear-bear.

Danielle Aucott (9)
St Peter's CE Primary School, Market Bosworth

My Dream Island

My dream island
Knows if it needs mowing
My dream island
Has a palm tree growing
My dream island
Can do sowing
My dream island
Has new birds crowing.

Fiona Naylor (8)
St Peter's CE Primary School, Market Bosworth

Weather

W eather can be fun and happy,
E ven when it rains.
A fter rain the best comes
T he sun comes out to play.
H ear the shouting, 'Hooray, hooray!'
E ither when it's sun or rain,
R ather sun any day.

Sabina Marr (8)
St Peter's CE Primary School, Market Bosworth

Honey Shopping

I have come to the garden shops today
Come to get some nectar,
Here is the sunflower glimmering and gay,
The buttercups, sun-bright yellow,
There is the lavender sparkling blue.
Roses, red as the bright sunset,
Cupping some glistening nectar.
Gently I land on the pretty flowers,
And scoop the splendid stickiness into my tiny pouch.
Now away I fly on my little, light wings,
Back to the honeycomb,
The little bees' pot for us to store our food.
Honeycombs are golden and dripping with shining honey.
Greedily we feed off the hexagons,
That is a bee's life!

Emily Roberts (8)
St Peter's CE Primary School, Market Bosworth

All Around The Haunted House

In the haunted house,
The floorboards *crack,*
And the door went *creak.*
The owl went *hoot,*
And the mouse went *squeak.*
In the bathroom,
The tap went *drop,*
And the bath went *splash!*
The cat by the sculpture knocked it,
Smash!
In the kitchen
The cat went *purr,*
And the pots went *bash.*
I sat on the chair and it fell down,
Crash!
In the living room,
The chair went *squash,*
And the fire went *click.*
The bird went *swoop,*
I went, quick as a *flick!*

Leah Croston (9)
Shrubland Street Community Primary School

The Haunted House

When I walked into a haunted house,
Tick, tock, tick, went the grandfather clock,
Drip, drop, drip, went the leak in the roof,
Creak, creak, creak, went the floorboards,
Snip, snap, snip, went the crocodile in the lake,
Howl, howl, howl, went the wolf in the forest,
Boo, boo, boo, went the ghost behind me,
Ha! Ha! Ha! Went the skeleton,
Whoosh, whoosh, whoosh, went the draught,
Hoot, hoot, hoot, went the owl in the tree,
Roar, roar, roar, went the pet lion,
Pop, pop, pop, went the bubbling cauldron,
Squeak, squeak, squeak went the aliens landing,
Swish, swish, swish, went Frankenstein's spanner,
Boom, boom, boom went the chair's legs,
Scratch, scratch, scratch, went the dog's flea circus,
And I got to be the leader!

Victoria Brown (10)
Shrubland Street Community Primary School

Drip, Drip, Drip

Drip, drip, drip,
Goes the tap, tap, tap,
And *tap, tap, tap,*
Goes the wind, wind, wind,
And *rustle, rustle, rustle,*
Goes the pipe, pipe, pipe,
And *creak, creak, creak,*
Goes the floor, floor, floor,
And *mumble, mumble, mumble,*
Goes the telly next door.

Jade Reeve (10)
Shrubland Street Community Primary School

In The Night

Howl; a wolf at full moon,
Swish; the grass on a windy night,
Creak; a rusty old door,
Hoot; an owl when it catches its prey,
Squeak; a mouse nestling down in a bed of leaves,
Scratch; a dog with a coat full of fleas,
Crash; a cat knocking down a dustbin,
Drip; a drop of water from a leaking drainpipe,
Snore; a man at 1 o'clock in the morning,
Cock-a-doodle-doo; a cockerel at the crack of dawn,
Silence is me
Just how I like it!

Rebekah Waterfield (9)
Shrubland Street Community Primary School

Tanka

Passing the long hour
With absolute precision,
Slowly, hands moving,
Every second and minute
Drawing us ever onwards.

Anja Bell (10)
Shrubland Street Community Primary School

I Remember

I remember my hamster
The way she burrowed
The way she played.

I remember the way
She spun her wheel
And scratched around.

I remember the way
She shredded up paper
And bit me for the first time.

I remember the way
She did the monkey bars
And played up my jumper.

I remember the way
She shoved lettuce in her pouches
And cuddled up to sleep.

I remember when she . . .

Didn't wake up.

Thomas Hood (10)
Shrubland Street Community Primary School

What Is Red?

Red is the colour of so many passions,
Love,
From the heart,
Anger,
From the head,
Pain,
From the body,
Loyalty,
From the friend,
Devil,
From the evil,
Jealousy,
From the mind,
Flames,
From the eyes,
Selfishness,
From yourself,
Rainbow,
From the joy of your heart,
Mysterious,
From the secrets,
And that's what I think about the colour *red!*

Harriet Bartle (11)
Shrubland Street Community Primary School

What Is Red?

Red is hot,
As the Devil
Burning red-hot,
Brightly bursting with envy
But . . . it is love,
Love, so rich and independent,
Love blinded by evil
Evil consumes all
To overcome it is to master it,
And to exploit it to the world
Is like sending it into battle
But . . . love will conquer all.

Joe Durrant (11)
Shrubland Street Community Primary School

Breakfast At Little Bear's House

Mummy went *snore, snore!*
Daddy's tummy went *grumble, grumble!*
Daddy got up and went *yawn, yawn!*
Daddy went downstairs going, *thump, thump!*
My cereal went *snap, crackle, pop!*
Daddy's breakfast went *sizzle, sizzle!*
My breakfast went in my mouth, *crunch, crunch!*
Little brother went *'Waaa! Waaa!'*
Little brother's rattle went *rattle, rattle!*
Uh oh, there's an icky smell.
Parp, parp!
Little brother!

Zac Chandler (10)
Shrubland Street Community Primary School

Gargoyles

Frozen demons,
Shadows of the past,
Mysterious presence,
Dead?

Twilight flyer,
Teeth sharp,
Villain?
Yet . . . beautiful,
Gargoyles are alive.

Joseph Kwasnik (11)
Shrubland Street Community Primary School

She Seeps Beauty

She is cold and icy,
She has a heart of ice,
She is top of the weather range,
As she seeps beauty.

Her cold aqua blood runs down her veins,
Her flowing hair is the winter wind,
She cries as the howling wind,
As she seeps beauty.

She lets her rug of cold fluff down in bits,
Her tears are the hail, that is frozen,
When she gets angry she stampedes down the mountain,
As she seeps beauty.

She is not chemicals,
For she is pure,
She is pure white,
The only real white,
As she seeps beauty.

She feeds her baby rain with the pure of white,
She trains it to fall on everyone when it is annoyed,
She loves her rain with cold icy love,
And she seeps beauty.

She is snow!

Siani Cox (11)
Shrubland Street Community Primary School

Thomas

His name was Thomas, I remember,
He was my cousin's son, you know,
Was he younger or older than me?
I don't remember.

He had a pea-green slide, I remember,
He was incredibly kind, you know,
Was his mother's name Debbie?
I don't remember.

He had a black felt hat, I remember,
He had blond hair, you know,
Did he let me wear the hat?
I don't remember.

He had nice teddies, I remember,
He let me cuddle them, you know,
Did I let him cuddle mine?
I don't remember.

He had soft arms, I remember,
He hugged me on the beach, you know,
Was it romantic?
I don't remember.

He was my best friend, I remember,
I haven't seen him since I was two, you know,
Does he remember me?
I hope so.

Rachel Hannah Brook (10)
Shrubland Street Community Primary School

Kennings

Swift silence,
Black shadow,
Glistening glimpse,
Balancing tail,
Beautiful mind,
Little present,
Dazzling dancer,
Huge caller,
Poor prey,
Killer claw,
Killer cat . . .
Cute cat?

Aneesha Doal (10)
Shrubland Street Community Primary School